THE MASTER KEY OF GIVING-BIRTH TO GREATER GENIUSES THROUGH GUIDED-PREGNANCIES

NURSE & NURTURE

BABY'S TALENTS BY PRE-NATAL & POST-NATAL EDUCATION

SUMMERIZED

SYNOPSIS

WISDOM IS THE ABILITY TO KNOW THE RIGHT THING TO DO AT THE RIGHT TIME IN THE RIGHT PLACE. WHAT EARTHLY MANKIND NEED TO ENABLE THEM DOWNLOAD THE LONGED-FOR KINGDOM OF HEAVEN, AS THE LORD'S PRAYER DEMANDS IS THE PREMISE OF THIS PUBLICATION. IN THISWISE, IT IS IMPERATIVE NECESSITY DEMANDS THAT THE WILLING, SERIOUS-MINDED AND WISE MOTHER OR MOTHER-TO-BE MUST KNOW HER ONOINS, WELL ENOUGH IN ADVANCE... TO AVOID FAUX PAR IN HER CHOICE OF THE INCARNATING HUMAN-SOUL AND ITS TALENTS, TRAITS (ADEQUACIES & INADEQUACIES) AIMS, MISION-GOALS AND WHAT IT STANDS TO ACHIEVE ON EARTH THROUGH HER PREGNANCY. EVERY BABY (GIRL OR BOY) COMES LOADED WITH TALENTS, AND A FEW CHOSEN-ONES WITH SPECIAL GIFTS FOR SPECIAL SERVICES TO HUMANITY AS GENIUSES.

MERE FAITH ALONE DOES NOT SUFFFICE TO ACCOMPLISH THIS ASPIRATION AND VALUED CONSTRUCTIVE ENGAGEMENT OF DOWNLOADING THE HEAVENLY REPLICA THROUGH NEW INVENTIONS TO THIS EARTH. FOR EXAMPLE, THE FOURTH INDUSTRIAL REVOLUTION, WHICH IS THE SO-CALLED CHAIN BLOCK INTERNET DEVING IS REALLY NEW. IT WILL CHECK AND CHECKMATE FRAUD AND FRAUDSTER IN BUSINESS AND GORVERNAMCE ACROSS THE WORLD IN OUR TIME.MORE WORK, ENDEAVORS AND ACCOMPLISHMENTS ARE REQUIRED. TO BEGIN WITH, THE HEREDITARY SIN, WHICH, WE UNDERSTAND, IS THE TRANSFER OF THE OVER-DEVELOPMENT OF THE FRONTAL-BRAIN(THE SEAT OF THE INTELLECT) TO THE DETRIMENT OF THE HIND-BRAIN(USED FOR SPIRITUAL RECEPTIVITY) TO THEIR BABIES RIGHT FROM THE WOMB MUST BE CORRECTED THROUGH AND DURING PREGNANCIES BY MOTHERS. AGAIN, THROUGH GUIDED PREGNANCIES, MOTHERS SHOULD MAKE THE BRINGING-FORTH OF GREATER GENIUSES THEIR

NECESSARY AND PREROGATIVE DUTY. SUCH GENIUSES , WHOSE INCARNATIONS ON EARTH WILL SERVE A GREAT FULFILLMENT OF THE INFINIT AND ETERNAL PROMISE OF THE COMING OF THE KINGDOM OF HEAVEN ON EARTH THROUGH GREAT WORKS. CONSIDER, IF FROM HINDSIGHT OF HISTORY, GENIUSES OF YESTER-CENTURIES , WITH THEIR DISTORTED AND UNEQUAL BRAIN COMPARTMENTS AND ABNORMAL FUNCTIONS,WERE ABLE TO ACCOMPLISH GREAT INVENTIONS AND DISCOVERIES WHICH WE ENJOY AT PRESENT, THEN GENIUSES WITH BALANCED BRAINS WILL ENGAGE AND UNDERTAKE GREATER ENDEAVORS AND DOWNLOAD NEW INVENTION S THAT WILL TRANSFORM THIS EARTH. TO PROFER THE NECSSARY ENLIGHTENMENT IN ORDER TO MAKE THIS IMPERATIVE CASE A FAITH ACCOMPLI IS THE CONCERN OF THIS BOOK.

TABLE *OF CONTENTS*

FOREWORD

IT must be true, inside the grave-yards lie wasted and forgotten the once highly-valued human-bodies that housed innumerable human-souls, bestowed and endowed with unimaginable and un-quantified magnitudes of un-used human talents; un-sung and unknown arts and acts of geniuses - due to non-recognition. Had mothers been rightly and timely informed, enlightened and supported on how to anchor, harvest and have better and greater geniuses through guided pregnancy, the longed-for Kingdom of God, as the perfect or Lord's Prayer demands, would have come to this earth long ago!

DEDICATION

This book is thoughtfully dedicated to wise mothers and mothers- to- be: Mothers, whose love for earthly mankind for better society is obvious!

PREFACE

CHILD-PSYCHOLOGISTS AND PAEDIATRICIANS agree in tandem, regarding baby's talents and geniuses; and said that every baby born to this world is a huge bundle of great talents, some of them geniuses in whom and through whom skills synergize and strategise with special great-callings, gifts and natural potentials.

This book, titled.."The Secret of Bringing-Forth Better & Greater Geniuses...and sub-titled - "BABY'S TALENTS:PRE-NATAL & POST-NATAL EDUCATION - MOTHER'S ROLE THROUGH GIUDED- PREGNANCIES AND BIRTH , advocates need for more geniuses in virtually all areas of human endeavors to transform this earth to a heavenly status. The new earth with her new agreeable humanity will soon enjoy the Age of Better & Greater

Geniuses...in the New Era – The Millenium. More new things to enjoy and more better true human-beings as it is in the Heavenly Kingdom, is no eutopian - dream. Take for instance, we have about 6,200 languages or ethno-cultural nationalities on earth. Most of these languages have been distorted through the excrescence of colonisation and are presently at the verge of extinction; most of them have no names for most things around and within their geo-historical and socio -cultural domains; needing over-haulig, updating and validation to sensitize, reorient and reintegrate their respective ethnic nationals. Anything that exists, but fails to keep a name is not known. And not used.This fate befalls most things today on this earth.To retrace and redress this malady requires the birth of geniuses who come with great endownments of the history, culture, geography and un-adultrated language of each tribe...and especially the linguistic geniuses for such dispossessed nationalities. And as it stands, the world, ie this earth needs, nearly three to six geniuses to work , upgrade and validate each language; implying a total of 18600 and 37200 geniuses to fix the earth's languages alone. Then you can imagine the strength and magnitude of the plea this simple book is soliciting for. You will add more grains of rich ideas by going through this verse from world ideas, especially if you're a young mother or mother- to- be. However, this book is for all women and girls of age.

INTRODUCTION

When it is said, men should respect and honor women and girls, the un-informed may not grasp the high intelligence and unmistakable rationale behind such demands. Latent with reasons is the understanding that the future, fate and destiny of the entire-world and its humanity really reposed on the direction and quality of activities brought to bear on mankind by women and girls through their very nature and pregnancy in every society. Mankind will earn and enjoy the huge harvests of adequacies from constructive engagements if they make bold to respect and honor women and girls, as the requisite standards for a noble humanity, and a matter of fact and urgency.

CHAPTER ONE

Definition of Talent & Genius

Talents are nothing less than the natural potentials or abilities that are inherent in a human being. Talents are more than mere human potentials which need little or no guidance to perform.Mothers should not under-rate the value of toys and sand-games which naturally fall to children's lot!

1

Genius

A GENIUS: A GREAT CHOSEN, HIGHLY-GIFTED AND DYNAMIC CREATIVE-THINKER:

He ranks very high on the cadre of great-minds, and taps from the **infinite intelligence** to shape the world as a general in his field of human endeavors! The genius aims at ultimate success, no failures! And he is either born great, or achieves greatness, because he comes with requisite and consequential pictures for performance. The Genius learns to stimulate his brains and intuition; and gets them to function on the high realms of frequencies for creative-thinking and exclusive achievements! Suffice it to say, that a genius is an exclusively gifted chosen-one to turn things round for the public good through his rare feats of achievements that sounds mythical and mystical!

The genius is not lazy, and shuns the lukewarm, derides all half-measures and probes deeper into his search with research and experiments. He can go on and on trying a thousand and one possible ways and means to reach his chosen Eldorado...

Instances abound!

THOMAS EDISON

Thomas Alvin Edison, otherwise, known as the Wizard of Menlo Park, California (USA) patented 60 inventions in his Itime; which Mr. Henry Ford, of Henry Ford Motor Manufacturing Corporation (U.S.A) described as The Age of Edison.

In 1925, he gave phonogram, to the world, after his recorded 1110th experiments that failed, then came the 1111th

SIR OLA-UDAH IKWU-ANO

Another genius, a Black, Sir Ola-Udah Ikwu-Ano, the Igbo slave-boy who bought his freedom from his master in Virginia, USA. He played a very active role in the Abolish Slave Trade through his book which depicted how 'ZONG', the slave ship callously jettisoned 133 slaves for the ship owners to claim insurance money, and demanded for immediate stoppage of slave trade from the British Lawmakers, Sir William Wilberforce and the Quakers stood behind Ikwu-Ano and gave ultimatum to the British Parliament for the uncontested promulgation of the Slave Trade Abolition Act of 1807

MICHAEL FARADAY

WE wonder how this world and human life would be without electricity! Michael Faraday helped the world to answer that question! Born 1791, Faraaday was one of the greatest English scientists – a chemist and physicist. He discovered the power of Electromagnetic Induction in 1831,

ALBERT EINSTEIN

There is need to mention more geniuses like Albert Einstein. German physicist, the man who made Relativity and Space-Time concept a household word! He says everything is relative. Einstein's simple strokes of mathematical fiat, put paid on his stand in 1905!

ISAAC NEWTON

Sir Isaac Newton gave scientific values to Gravity, Motion, Dispersion of the Seven Colors from White Light and more; generally referred to as the Laws of Gravity, The Three Laws of Motion and The Laws of Spectrometry, among others.

LEONADO DA VINCCI

Leonardo Da Vinci, Italian great-mind! A poet, musician, philosopher, great inventor - bicycle, helicopter, (automatic unmanned vehicle) the armoured-vehicle, scud missile, mentioned the possibility of space journey, etc.

MICHAEL JACKSON

WORLD-CLASS POP SINGER and U.S-based music genius, Michael Jackson qualified for a global brand name, like coke and Marlboro, according to Richard Bernet and John Cavanagh in their

GALILEO GALILEI(1564-1642)

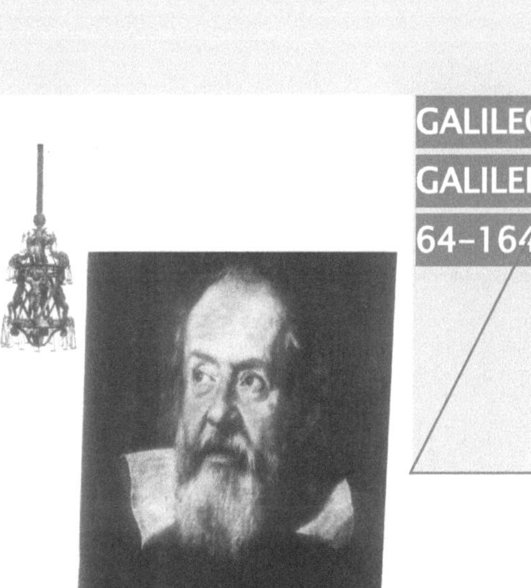

WIZARD OF PISA, AVID STAR-GASER; GARNERRED THE MASTERY OF THE MIRRORS & DEVELOPED THE LENSES AND INVENTED THE FOREMOST TELESCOPE THAT ENABLED HIM TO PROVE THE CHURCH WRONG . THE CHURH OF ROME HELD SWAY THAT THE EARTH WAS FLAT LIKE TABLE. BUT GALILEO SAID NO! THE EARTH IS ROUND AND IT HAS BEEEN PROVED TO BE TRUE

the president of the Holy Court of Inquisition of the Holy Roman Empire, and the uncontesred hammer of the Catholic heretics)June 23, 1633... he said, during the eclipse of the moon, the reflected shadow of the earth is cast on the sun, and it is round.'Only a round object can cast a round shadow, therefore, the earth,I affirm, is round,but not flat' - G And to Robert Cardinal Bellarmin(ALILEO!

Cardinal Bellarmin was dump-folded

JOHN HARRISON

John Harrison, the man who captured the mystery of time

in time-contrap, an instrument for measuring time, otherwise known as the Clock! Harrison was said to have taken fire for his invention from Gallileo's previous discovery on the use of the Pendulum - juxtaposed in the synergy of the heart-beats and the pendulum ossilations. Gallileo assigned the an interval of a successive heart-beat to one second, from which Harrison later derives his unit of time in the invention of the Clock

Mahathma Ghandi

Freed India from British 400-year cololnial rule through non-violence protests and demonstrations, among others.

CHAIRMAN MAO Tse-Tung and PM CHOU E n-Lai

The two compatriot makers of the great modern China! They truly made China shine! Mao and Chou brought China together, made them one and great through their disciplinary and dominant austerity measure, with…a very strict stance, "do not bring any foreign items into China and do not take away any indigenous item there-from.

EDWARD QUEEN ALEXANDRINA VICTORIA

QUEEN VICTORIA EDWARD

Victoria Alexandrina Edward ascended the Throne as the Queen of The United Kingdom at 18, and ruled for 63 years, seven months non-stop. And she made Britain great! It was during the Victorian Era that the United Kingdom climaxed the height of Industrial Revolution its peak in Industrial Revolution during the Victorian
epoch; even though a woman.

She has her name etched as great and remarkable ornaments on monuments in many nations, around the world. The name "Victoria" rings bells in places like: Lake Victoria .

Robert Nesta Marley

BOB MARLEY

MARLEY Robert Nesta Otherwise, known as Bob Marley, was born in Jamaica on February 6, 1945. He was the rhythm guitarist and lead singer of Bob Marley & the by storm as the Wailers, his musical band with which he took the world by by surprise;great musician, peot, song writer, philosopher, a soldier-activist and leader. Bob Marley, no doubts, put his naïve Island, Jamaica on the world map as the country with the greatest indigenous export of Reggae music in the world.

GEORGE WASHINGTON(1732-1799)

WASHINGTON GEORGE, father of US-Natiionalism.

Washington was the first President of the United States of America. He did not start school until he was 14 or 15.

NICCOLO MARCHIAVELLI

The name Machiavelli evokes deep darkness in all equations and eandeavors! For him, nothing is sacrosanct!

AMERIGO DE VESPUCCI (1451-1512)

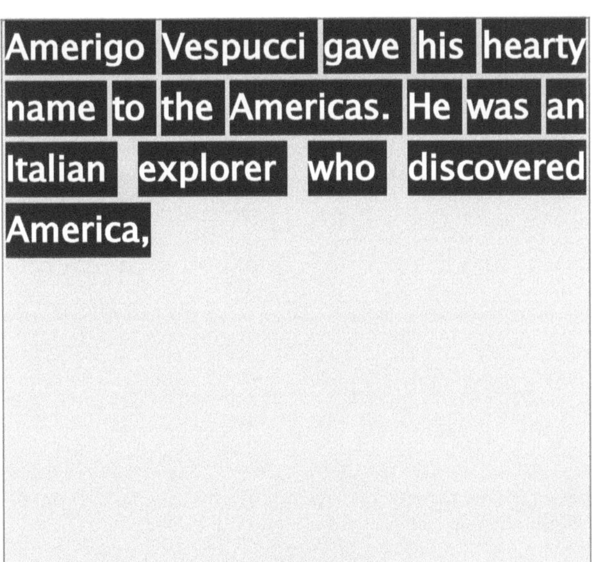

CHAPTER TWO

Thy Kingdom Come: Mother's Role!

THE LORD'S PRAYER anchors the possibility of the kingdom come to this ea of the Almighty-Creator to rth, so that we may have and host a replica of the Heavens down here!

But how! We need to develop this earth to reflect the splendours and unimaginable beauty that don and adorn heaven to grace this earth!

Look, it's not going to end with sending of good-will alone! Aah! Prayer is important, yet work is also very much imperative necessity!

You know what! His earth needs more talented workers a great flood of geniuses to transform it into the longed-for Kingdom of heaven!

Mothers have lofty roles to play! Through guided pregnancy, more geniuses will be born!

CHAPTER THREE

Before Marriage

Long before marriage , a young woman or a girl who contemplates having children, becomes the lot of most women, it is adviseable to ask yourself the kind of child r children you intend to host,
A would-be mother should make a duty to decide and determine this matter objective! It is not funny!

Why there are much evil population of humans on earth today could be because mothers never planed procrattion and pregnancy beforehand long prior to marriage! Long before you think of taking in, ask yourself the simple question ...'Who's coming through this pregnancy, who am I bringing into this world and what is it coming to do!

CHAPTER FOUR

Prior to Pregnancy:
The Necessary Prayers to The Most-High
& The Requisite Conditions

PREGNANCY is the response to the gift of nature by the woman, who considers it due and worthwhile, to conceive and develop a human-body for an incarnating human-soul from the world-beyond to use for earthly existence and experience.

First of all, one needs give thanks to the Most High for protection, guidance and fulfilment, both for mother and the incarnating-soul (the expected-baby),

And like someone who aims a catching a fish sea, one needs a hook and sincker with a requisite bait. The expectant-mother should send her strong wish with a specific area of endeavour and achievement into the world-beyond. She must continue to nourish that strong volition until the human-soul incarnates into her womb, we now know, at the middle of pregnancy.

The requisite conditions are:

There is no substitute for womanliness for wholesome pregnancy. Genius comes from regions of Light...has nothing to do with the regions of Darkness.

You must be truly disciplined to be humble, and morally sound! If you fail discipline, morality and humility tests, you may not be simple and open enough to receive anything from the Light-Regions, not even a genius!

You must not compromise respectable good lifestyle. Above all, avoid any polluted lifestyle, remain inwardly clean and also outwardly kempt! Also make real prayer youe second nature in goodwill!

CHAPTER FIVE

The Incarnating Human-Soul: From Where...?

The incarnating human soul: From where, is questionable.

The incarnating human-soul comes from any plane of existence that is not visible by the earthly eyes, ears, and other senses of the earthly human-body!

I see! Now if the world-beyond is consistent with those planes of existence, where one's earthly senses cannot see, hear or feel anything, how then was it possible for those who claim the existence of this purported world-beyond planes able to source their proofs? It begs concise clarity and conviction.

Fine enquiry! You're a very good student of life! Now tell me, are you aware that your earthly body is not you? That the real you is inside your earthly body - and that is your soul, who claims "my body, my eyes, my car, my wife, my husband, my this and my that...

We sleep, yetstill find our- sleep and selves very active far afrom our sleeping place where way

The earthly-body has its sense organs, ourearthly bodies reposed abed, fast asleep. That's a very good conscious observation!

The physical has its sesnse , and the soul-body also its own sense organs. With the earthly senses, earthman sees earthly things, the same way the human-soul(man outside his earthly physical-body) sees , or hears the supra-earthly things with the sense-organs of his soul-body!

Let us reason together! When we sleep, our body lies down on the bed, but we see ourselves busy as we do in day time. Now tell me, the plane where we see ourselves active like we do during day-consciousness, is it earth-plane?

Definitely no! That plane belongs to a section in the world-beyond!

You get it roundly!

CHAPTER SIX

Pre-Natal & Post-Natal Education: An Imperative Necessity For Every Expectant Mother

(Post -natal education)

Pre-Natal and Post-Natal Education! These are two diverse ways, means and manners of speaking to a baby while still developing and maturing inside the womb, towards earthly birth, psycho-medically referred to as pre- natal education; on one hand, complementary to the art of enlightening the new-born baby, immediately after earthly birth, outside its mother's womb, otherwise known as post-natal education, on the other hand!

ie, her strong will-power waves issuing from her own soul) contain the messag (e (in form of pictures without words) which she wants to convey to her baby! And the baby on its side is very sensitive to both external and internal vibrations around it. Mind you, the baby's soul-body contains very powerful spiritual organs, which enable it (depending on the spiritual personality of the incarnating-soul) to feel, see(the pictures), hear and absorb the vibration of the mother's strong wishes or volitions, laden with the message that assails it...!

There is truth in the foregoing, because it has logic! The iron in the foundry & smith chamber takes any shape, according to the wishes or volitions directed to it!

Pre-Natal Education!

Imagine a friend of yours from a foreign land is making moves to visit you for the first time. He will count on you as his best friend, if you inform and educate him about your country before he makes his foremost landing.

Post-Natal Education

Even after successfully making his first-time entry into you country, you still owe him some good responsibility of tutoring him on the nitty-gritty about your peoples and places(if your country is a multi-ethnic society), life, activities, the Laws, Bye-Laws, Rules & Regulations, adequacies and inadequacies, more especially in this terror and corruption polluted world, capped with shamelessness, so that from the very beginning, he stands on familiar grounds, armed with point-and-click understanding of the new environment...in order to avoid every danger, rather, he will triumph over his purpose of visit, and suffused with joy and true happiness. And his triumph and success is also yours at the end!

These analogies proffer us with some vivid pictures to reflect pre-natal and post-natal ways of educating the baby before and immediately after birth!

That's good

CHAPTER SEVEN

Europe & Geniuses: Modern Civilization – The Age Of Renaissance & Reasoning

The truth in the saying that the modern world borrowed the fire of development from Europe leaves no room for contention. It's unarguable! Modern Civilization, which came to lime-light in Europe started with Age of Renaissance & Reasoning, between 1400 A.D., to the present Era, saw Europe leading the world virtually in all ranks of human specialties in their endeavors

It's a lie! 1400A.D. falls short in place and could not have belonged to The Modern Era... That date in history, in the March of Civilization and Human Development on earth belongs to the Medieval or Middle-Ages.

ROBERT BOYLE

Robert Boyle, a man of chemistry, in the Age of Reasoning and Renaissance)

Robert Boyle, for instance, was referred to as the leading figure in the march of modern chemistry, because of the leading roles he played during the Age of Reaasoning and The Reniassance in the the Meeval Europe!

HIPPOCRITUs

One good proof to support the fact that modern civilization took fire from the ancients and antiquities was evident in the works of the Greek Philosopher and Alchemist, Hippocritus. He was reported to be the first to mention and show enough proofs that all things are made of atoms!

I see! Who is an Alchemist?

Like the word implies, an alchemist is one who dared ancient methods of heating base-metal to obtain precious stones like gold, silver, emerald, diamond. etc. Alchemy is ancient chemistry, whence modern chemistry derives! Hippocritus laid the foundation of chemistry of all times through his foremost knowledge of atoms. Today, atomicity is chemistry! Indeed, no atoms, no chemistry!

MICHAELANGELO BOUNARROTI(1475-1564)

Michaelangelo, one man who made remarkable landmark in the developement of sculpture and painting arts . He remains very relevant in the cadre of great minds! Not only one of the most famous artists in history, he was a great leader of the Italian Renaissance.

Angelos was remarkably interested in creating large marble statues. In addition, he was a great sculptor, an architect and a poet!

One of his greatest large marble statues shows the Virgin Mary sited, carrying the dead body of her murdered son - Lord Jesus Christ after the Crucifixion .

To bring these great minds of chosen and highly gifted men and women to mothers' foremost role in the development of this earth!

Can this feat still be achieved today!

Creation can make use of any human-mothers to fulfill this high promise as long as she is willing

CHAPTER EIGHT

Grave-Yards Belly Un-Used Great Talents, Un-Song Geniuses

The Trappings from Over-Pampered Dunces

BELIEVE IT or not, unimaginable multitudes of un-used great talents, un-song geniuses and the trappings of over-pampered dunces are bellied in grave-yards daily all over the world!

That sounds true!

But are you a genius?

I do not know!

Then you may not know if you fall into the caste of the over-pampered dunces!

What if I belong to the talent-world!

When you're not sure of yourself, because your mother did not care about your talents! You fall short in place of the great saying...'Man know thyself!"

What about you, did your mother dare to know your innate traits! Most mothers run short of appresal and failed in their maternal duties to their children and humanity, because they have never bordered to identify their children's talents, much less if they were geniuses.!

Perhaps, by examining this presentation, mothers may sue for a change and introduce geniuses afresh to invent and discover new things for enjoyment of, and joy for humanity!
It's a pity that the splendid works of most talents and geniuses intended for the development of a valued humanity in this part of Creation are wasted to ignorance and obscurity...in the graves!

And what have you to say about the over-pampered dunces? Just be candid enough!

Though their talents and the work of ingenuities they came to accomplish failed; un-used, un-song , and unknown; willing-mothers can still recast the geniuses afresh through new guided-pregnancies!

CHAPTER NINE

URGENT NEED TO FASHION NORMAL HUMAN-BRAINS: THE FRONTAL-BRAIN & THE BACK-BRAIN BECOME EQUAL

BOTH IN SIZE & FUNCTIONS

THIS NEWBREED OF BRAINS
- A PLUS FOR A TRUE HUMANITY
THAT WILL FLOOD THIS EARTH
WITH BETTER & GREATER GENIUSES
TO REPLICATE THE LONGED-FOR
KINGDOM OF HEAVEN

BIOLOGISTS AND HEALTH-WORKERS alike, know that the human-brain has two unequal compartments - the frontal-brain and the hind-brain: Biology grouped them that way as it pleased biology! It calls the frontal-brain the cerebrum and names the back-brain the cerebelum

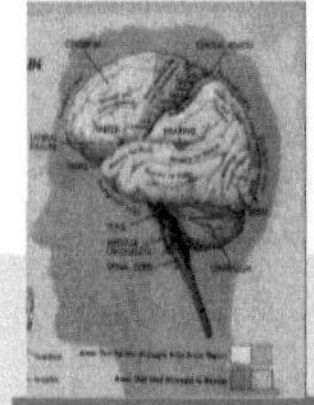

(The hunman brain, the (red) frontal portion, and the seat of intellect, which is the cerebrum is disproportionately larger than the (dark-red) hind portion, otherwise referred to as the cerebellum.)

We are made to understand that the frontal brain is used for earthly understanding and activities, whereas, the hind brain receives impressions of true spiritual knowledge from the World-Beyond, and pass them to the frontal brain for earthly applications,This natural synergy between the two parts of the human brain ensues the requisite harmony that will engage and engender a replication of the Kingdom of Heaven if mothers bring-forth geniuses with brains of equal frontal and hind portions to play in their new inventions and discoveries.

Comment [IO]:

Comment [IO]:

Flooding the earth with greater and better geniuses through guided pregnancies; by earliest approach to educating the baby in line with the use of pre-natal and post-natal education during pregnancy and immediately after the baby successfully arrived is not enough to anchor that longed-for Kingdom of Heaven on earth; rather, being able to develop human-babies with frontal and hind parts of the brain equal in size and function, is very much imperative a necessity now!

From a High Source of world ideas, we now understand how Lucifer, the Fallen Arch-Angel changed the Great Apple of Spiritual Qualities which the Amighty-Creator of all bestowed in woman. How verything thatwas meant for the development of this earth and its mankind, consigned to woman was ruined by inability to exercise her great power of intuition to resist Lucifer's prompting by the foremost human couples,on warth, collectively referred to as Eve and Adam. And of course, Eve and Adam were warned not to taste of the knowledge of life(because they had to develop and mauture for its use), Lucifer, coming from his Height was sent by the Creator to help in their proper development on earth, But he lacked patience!

He awakened the charm of high ideas in Eve prematurely, and unable to control it, she turned it into the charm of vanity!

Eve sold her new awakening to Adam (the first-batch of human-man on earth). And he bought it (without **money**) because it satisfied their curiosity.

Adam, on the other decided to protect and please Eve by accumulating things of material values, acquiring and surrounding her with material treasures,, to balance his exploitation of the woman's charm of vanity! Later they developed greed which they applied jealously; the A & O of all evils...the excrescences of Lucifer's Wrong Principle!

The Acquisition and accumulation of materials is functional with the frontal brain, to the neglect of the hind brain. The prolonged use and over-use of the frontal brain enlarged it disproportionately in size and function to the detriment of the hind brain which suffered atrophy due to un-usage for millions of years. Woman transferred her sin of charm of vanity to posterity.

today, she fashions babies (by her calling of pregnancy) that have huge frontal brain and very tiny hind brain.the prospect, we understand is that such a baby will never connect to or concern itself with the spiritual heights for any spiritual vibrations, as it develops and matures. it will only concern itself with the materials! and that is how is it has been for millennia on earth, besides the alleged religious fundamentalism and evangelism!

As for the Serpent offering a forbidden apple to Eve, as was depicted in the Bible; that picture is right, yet is scores below the actual event of that narration by the Great Prophet. Lucifer wrongly activated powerful but destructive current from the woman's generative-base, which flowed through her Spinal-Cord to her brain in a snaky form and polluted her senses,.. the apple of her great endowment and bestowment which she suppose to preserve and protect till it was time to put them to wise and profitable use!

It was the flow of the deceptive energy-current from Lucifer through the curves of the woman's back-back bone , which inscribed the depicted evil-fated Serpent of intellectual sacrilege!

But Eve, being a woman had all it took to prevent Lucifer from taking her un-awares. That was her failure and great sin which she allowed to become hereditary upon posterity. Through woman the havoc of wrong development of the human-brain was manifest, and again, through woman, the wound of the hereditary sin will heal if, and only if mothers make bold and play the low-key in this matter.

Long before any pregnancies, any wise woman who aspires bringing-forth a child should first thank the Lord-Almighty for everything and ask for forgiveness of the hereditary sin, for herself and on behalf of the entire earthly humanity for all times since the beginning of the wrong development of the human brain by the first bach of the by-gone earthly womanhood through her unfortunate and unforgatable joint destructive engagements.

She should engage herself in serious heart-felt prayers consistently, and ask for help through the Grace and Mercy of the Most High so that the frontal and the hind parts of the new baby's brain during her anticipated new pregnancy will be equal during its formation in her womb! Immediately the mother becomes aware that she has taken in, she should make it a habit, touching her pregnancy from time to time and urging the Nature-Forces and Nature-Beings who partake in the fashioning of the baby's boby in the womb to help and fashion the baby's brain to have the frontal and hind parts of the brain equal in size and function.

Parent(s) and guidians should always remember what they implored and asked for in a child prior to pregnancy, and make sure the child's upbringing and training flows accordingly.

FORWARD

FROM past millennia, world peoples with diverse cultures and traditions have had varied means and ways of diving the person who has incarnated or reincarnated into their homes.

In most cases, their methods compromise occultism, diabolism, witchcraft and sorcery; with their attendant make-beliefs and errors by dupes who claim medium-ship, but are not!

The author intends more than that!

The secret of anchoring, and having geniuses, as the title of this book implies, transcends the above-listed means and ways. It addresses the expectant mother to know before-hand the nature and qualities of the incarnating-human soul during pregnancy. It requires neither divination nor triangulation investigation methods.

BLURB

A mother or mother-to-be will be doing humanity a sumptuous good if she can make bold, but humbly to examine the rich exploits of this inspiring book

Prof. Ben Ezeohagwu

ACKNOWLEGMENT

My humble acknowledgement goes to Ms Success Okani, Professor Ben Ezeohagwu, and to any other persons who in one way or the other, served a good means to this lofty end: Who strongly believe in the unassailable fact that the content determines the quality, and also, the means justifies the end, and not vice versa!

KAHAMMA RUTEMMA +2348121524312

: KAHAMMA RUTEMMA

Book References

Britain and the Beast
PETER HOWARD
The Mystery of Time:
Humanities Quest for Order and Measure
JOHN LANGONE(NATIIONL GEOGRAPHIC)
Keys to the Deeper Life
JOHN WESLEY
(REVISED AND EXPANDED BY A,W, TOZER)
Strategies
For Improving Your Intelligence and Connections
How greatest inventors, writers, and leaders used sleep, swimming, sex and music to boost their brain)
ONYIMA JUDE KC
The Bible
KING JAMES VERSON
The Qu'ran
KING FAHD VERSION
The Grail Message
(IN THE LIGHT OF TRUTH)
ABD-RU-SHIN

www.ingramcontent.com/pod-product-compliance
Ingram Content Group UK Ltd.
Pitfield, Milton Keynes, MK11 3LW, UK
UKHW041904190726
13854UKWH00003B/1077

9 780359 069811